TO:

_____

FROM:

_____

DATE:

_____

A NOTE:

the POWER
OF A WISE
WOMAN

EDDIE LONG

J COUNTRYMAN

Nashville, Tennessee
www.jcountryman.com

Copyright ©2002 by Eddie Long.

Published by J. Countryman®, a division of Thomas Nelson, Inc.,
Nashville, Tennessee 37214

J. Countryman® is a trademark of Thomas Nelson, Inc.

Unless otherwise indicated, all Scripture quotations in this book are from the New
King James Version® (NKJV) © 1979, 1980, 1982, 1992,
Thomas Nelson, Inc. Publisher.

Designed by DeAnna Pierce, The Office of Bill Chiaravalle, Sisters, OR
www.officeofbc.com
Project Editor: Kathy Baker

ISBN 0-8499-9650-3

Printed and bound in Belgium

www.thomasnelson.com

TABLE *of* CONTENTS

The VALUE of WISDOM

Whoever is wise

will observe these things,

And they will understand

the lovingkindness

of the Lord.

PSALM 107:43

WISDOM *is the* POWER *of* GOD *at* WORK *in* HUMAN LIVES.

But who is supposed to hold that wisdom? God gives freely, of course, but I believe it is the major gift meant for women of the Kingdom.

The writer of Proverbs commands,

"Get wisdom! Get understanding! . .
Wisdom is the principal thing;
therefore get wisdom . . .
exalt her [wisdom] and she will promote you;
she will bring you honor . . ."

PROVERBS 4:5, 7–8.

Isn't it interesting that in the book of Proverbs, beginning in chapter 8 the writer refers to wisdom as a *woman*?

There's no denying that everyone in the church—men, women, children, even pastors—needs the power possessed by wise women. And such power doesn't stop at the church-house door. It flows on out into the community, impacting schools, neighborhoods, even world leaders.

You think I'm exaggerating? The Bible is replete with examples like Jochebed, Deborah, Ruth, Abigail, Esther, and Mary. All of these women changed the course of history, simply by being wise in how they faithfully handled their circumstances.

And isn't it interesting that so many wise woman—like the wise woman of Tekoa—are never called by name? The reason, I believe, is that God wanted the spotlight to shine on what they *did* instead of telling the world who they *were*. The Bible refers to more than seven hundred thirty women in the Bible who remained unnamed. This fact may mean that some wise women may say the right words, speak the truth, and yet may never be praised, honored, or exalted. Part of wisdom is to realize that although a woman might not get human recognition, God knows, and God will one day reward her.

We see a variety of stories in the Bible of the powerful wisdom of women, even when they're not named or specifically called wise. Keep reading and I'll show you. There are a thousand different ways to be wise, but I'm going to break it down real simple into how wisdom impacts three kinds of relationships—with God, with other people, and with yourself.

Wisdom is key to women claiming the power that God intended for them to have. In this book I am laying down the principles of wisdom that God has given to woman so that she can be who God has ordained—in raising a family, in enhancing and building up man, in enhancing her own life and being able to walk in her true destiny. It is my prayer to revolutionize a woman's thinking and cause her to find out everything God intended for her to have. If she walks in the womanhood that God ordained for her to walk in, then everybody connected with that woman will be blessed.

Knowledge comes

but wisdom lingers.

ALFRED TENNYSON

English poet (1809-1892)

BEING WISE *in* RELATIONSHIP *with* GOD

If God is slow in

answering your request,

and you ask

but do not promptly

receive anything

do not be upset,

for you are not wiser than God.

ABRAHAM OF NATHPAR
(early seventh century)

A S a CHILD *of* GOD,
DIVINELY CREATED
to GLORIFY HIM,

a woman's primary relationship is her relationship with God. You can get by without anything else, but a relationship with the Father is essential. If you're reading this book, I'm guessing that you know this.

So how do you be wise in your relationship with an all-powerful, all-knowing Creator, especially since "the foolishness of God is wiser than man's wisdom, and the weakness of God is stronger than man's strength" (1 Corinthians 1:15)?

You start by trusting Him.

Is He God? Yes.
Are you? No.

Trust Him. Get to know Him.

"The fear of the Lord is the beginning of wisdom,
And the knowledge of the Holy One is understanding"
(Proverbs 9:10).

Build your relationship on trust and you'll see how He loves you, how He takes care of you, and how He can use you in His Kingdom.

Take a look at several women's relationships with God. Jochebed, Hannah, and Mary all trusted God, and the more they trusted, the more He delivered. On the other hand, the examples of Sarah and Sapphira show us what happens when women don't trust God enough.

17 Incline your ear and hear the words of the wise,

And apply your heart to my knowledge;

18 For it is a pleasant thing if you keep them within you;

Let them all be fixed upon your lips,

19 So that your trust may be in the LORD;

I have instructed you today, even you.

20 Have I not written to you excellent things

Of counsels and knowledge,

21 That I may make you know the certainty

of the words of truth,

That you may answer words of truth

To those who send to you?

PROVERBS 22:17-21

JOCHEBED

She Put Her Child into God's Hands

If this woman's name doesn't ring a bell with you, it's been too long since you were in a Sunday school class for little children.

Jochebed was the mother of Moses. She and the rest of the children of Israel were going through some tough times in Egypt. Whereas their families had once been welcomed back in Joseph's day, now they were slaves. Even worse, Pharaoh was afraid of the Hebrews' continued strength, so he "commanded all his people, saying, 'Every son who is born you shall cast into the river, and every daughter you shall save alive'" (Exodus 1:22).

Despite Pharoah's decree, Jochebed couldn't bring herself to harm her baby, so she hid him in her home. "But when she could no longer hide him, she took an ark of bulrushes for him, daubed it with asphalt and pitch, put the child in it, and laid it in the reeds by the river's bank. And his sister stood afar off, to know what would be done to him" (Exodus 2:3-4).

You know what happened next. The princess, Pharaoh's daughter, saw baby Moses, realized his plight, and decided to keep him.

Sister Miriam—a slave girl with some nerve—approached the royal bathers and ended up getting the princess *to pay* the baby's own mother to nurse him. "So the woman took the child and nursed him. And the child grew, and she brought him to Pharaoh's daughter, and he became her son" (Exodus 2:9-10).

Jochebed made the best of an impossible situation. She took care of Moses as long as she could, then set her baby afloat in the river—technically obeying Pharaoh—and posted Miriam to report back in case God worked a miracle. When the miracle came, Jochebed and Miriam were ready. Later, when Moses grew old enough, Jochebed again gave away her son, trusting that God would take care of the boy.

Jochebed's wisdom lay in her trust in the Lord and especially in being ready for His miracles. That motherly wisdom was the first step to leading the Hebrews out of Egypt.

Was it easy? Of course not! Jochebed gave her son everything that she could, then gave him up—twice. Both times she knew she'd probably never see him again, but she put her precious child into God's hands. And Moses received a destiny bigger than anything she could ever have dreamed.

Ladies, are you preparing your children for a big destiny? Are you counting on your own plans or God's?

At some point, every mother has to let her child go. Are you doing everything you can for your kids, then trusting God to hold them? Do you trust Him to hold *you*? Are you ready for His miracles?

21 *The wise in heart will be called prudent,*

And sweetness of the lip

increases learning.

22 *Understanding is a wellspring of life*

to him who has it.

But the correction of fools is folly.

23 *The heart of the wise teaches his mouth,*

And adds learning to his lips.

PROVERBS 16:21-23

HANNAH

She Held Nothing Back

Hannah wanted a baby more than anything. For years, she prayed faithfully to the Lord for a child, but her womb stayed closed. Finally, she promised God that if she had a son, then he would be dedicated to His service. God heard her prayer, and Samuel was born.

"Now when she had weaned him, she . . . brought the child to Eli. And she said, 'O my lord! As your soul lives, my lord, I am the woman who stood by you here, praying to the LORD. For this child I prayed, and the LORD has granted me my petition which I asked of Him. Therefore I also have lent him to the LORD; as long as he lives he shall be lent to the LORD'" (1 Samuel 1:24-28).

Hannah loved this child of promise, but she valued her relationship with God even more. She kept her word to Him and entrusted her son to His keeping. The Lord blessed her with five more children, but every year she made her firstborn a little robe and gave it to him when her husband came to offer an annual sacrifice.

Hannah's story is not an example of how to bargain with God for what you want. Instead, it's a picture of God's love and mercy toward those who trust Him. Hannah held nothing back from God, and in her vulnerability to Him, she made herself open to receive His abundant blessings.

Everything that you have is a precious gift from God. What are you holding back from Him? Are you blocking the door to new blessings? Open your heart, Hannah, and open yourself to receive more than you could have hoped for.

33 *Hear instruction and be wise,*

And do not disdain it.

34 *Blessed is the man*

who listens to me,

Watching daily at my gates,

Waiting at the posts of my doors.

35 *For whoever finds me finds life,*

And obtains favor from the LORD.

PROVERBS 8:33-35

[MATTHEW 1, 2, 12:46-50, 13:55-56, 27:56; MARK 3:31-35, 6:3, 15:40; LUKE 1:26-2:34, 2:41-50, 8:19-21; JOHN 2:1-12, 19:25-27; ACTS 1:14]

MARY

God Trusted Her with His Greatest Gift

Mary had one of the toughest assignments of anyone in history—she had to help God grow up. Think about it, the angel Gabriel offered her the job as a teenager, and she was still at it thirty-four years later when her child ascended into Heaven.

Do you think God would have entrusted this assignment to a woman who didn't have wisdom? She definitely was going to need it.

Let's look here. When the angel came to tell Mary the plan, she only asked one question—"how's this going to happen." She didn't get bogged down in "are you sure?" "why me?" "what are people going to think of me?" or "can we rethink this a little?" No, Mary got her question answered and said, "Behold the maidservant of the Lord! Let it be to me according to your word" (Luke 1:38). She trusted God, and she accepted His plan for her life.

But she also knew her limitations. She knew that she needed a little love and support from an older, wiser woman, so she "went into the hill country with haste, to a city of Judah, and entered the house of Zacharias and greeted Elizabeth. And it happened, when Elizabeth heard the greeting of Mary, that the babe leaped in her womb; and Elizabeth was filled with the Holy Spirit. Then she spoke out with a loud voice and said, 'Blessed are you among women, and blessed is the fruit of your womb! . . . Blessed is she who believed, for there will be a fulfillment of those things which were told her from the Lord'" (Luke 1:39–45). Mary's holy pregnancy was still a secret, but her cousin affirmed what the angel had told her. If Mary had had any doubts, now they were gone. She could do this!

Mary knew it wouldn't be easy, though. An unmarried girl showing up pregnant? Her reputation was shot even though God's angel convinced her fiancé to stand by her. She had to travel to Bethlehem while heavy with child, then give birth in a stable with no loved ones around except Joseph. A few days later, she had to make another trip— this time to Jerusalem—where an old man named Simeon

1 *The wise woman builds her house,*
But the foolish
pulls it down with her hands.
2 *He who walks in his uprightness*
fears the LORD,
But he who is perverse in his ways
despises Him.
3 *In the mouth of a fool*
is a rod of pride,
But the lips of the wise
will preserve them.

PROVERBS 14:1-3

picked up her child, spoke of His destiny, then told Mary that "a sword will pierce through your own soul" (Luke 2:35). To top it off, the young family soon had to flee to Egypt and live among strangers until it was safe to go home.

At some point, Mary finally settled into a normal life with Joseph in Nazareth. She raised Jesus and His younger brothers and sisters, and we can only imagine what she went through taking care of her household. Every mother needs wisdom in raising her children to maturity, and sometimes it's hard not to play favorites. But I can't help but wonder how Mary handled her kids—she had at least seven— knowing that her oldest child had a holy destiny. Luke tells us that she kept a lot stored in her heart, which to me shows her wisdom in holding her tongue and being discreet.

We also know that Mary gave Jesus a little push toward His public ministry when she asked him to provide more wine for the wedding in Cana. Soon afterward, she had to give Him up full-time to His work: "Then His mother and brothers came to Him, and could not approach Him because of the crowd. And it was told Him by some, who said, 'Your mother and Your brothers are standing outside, desiring to see You.' But He answered and said to them, 'My mother and My brothers are these who hear the word of God and do it'" (Luke 8:19-21). I believe that this is when Mary really started realizing that anyone who loved her Son was part of her family. She could have resented this seeming rejection, but instead she and her other children were drawn more deeply into His ministry and purpose.

The next time we see Mary with her Son is at the cross. She watches her baby suffer. They gaze at each other, both in unbearable pain. Her assignment was almost over. She'd cared for Him, sacrificed for Him, and rooted for Him since the angel came to her. But even there at the cross, their precious relationship was high on Jesus' priority list. "When Jesus therefore saw His mother, and the disciple whom He loved standing by, He said to His mother, 'Woman, behold your son!' Then He said to the disciple, 'Behold your mother!' And from that hour that disciple took her to his own home" (John 19:26-27). Why didn't Jesus entrust His mother to one of His brothers or sisters? We don't know. But it shows to me Mary's wisdom that she didn't question Him on that. She accepted. The mother was now obedient to her Child of promise, as she had been obedient to the God who sent Him to her.

We know the story. We know Mary's relationship with her Son wasn't over. Although we don't read that she actually witnessed His ascension, I believe she was there, because right after it, the disciples were together again in the upper room, where they "continued with one accord in prayer and supplication, with the women and Mary the mother of Jesus, and with His brothers" (Acts 1:14). It was a great family time.

Mary's power was in her obedience. She faithfully did the best she could in raising Jesus. She trusted God when the way was confusing, which it often was. She did more than just *following* God's will—she *followed through* on His will all the way to the end. She endured upheaval and ugliness, she was faithful in the "normal" times with her "normal" kids, and she continued her role as the Lord's maidservant by mothering the rest of the disciples even after Jesus was gone.

Sisters, it takes wisdom from the heart of God to live like that.

15 See then that you

walk circumspectly,

not as fools but as wise,

16 redeeming the time,

because the days are evil.

17 Therefore do not be unwise,

but understand what

the will of the Lord is.

EPHESIANS 5:15-17

SARAH & SAPPHIRA

So Close, But Sometimes So Far

Now, one can only hope that your relationship with God will grow in wisdom and beauty all your life, but most of us can expect some setbacks.

It's hard to trust all the time.

Take Sarah, for instance. She knew of God's promise to make her husband the father of a vast nation, but when she was in her seventies, she gave up on God making her the mother. Sarah then pushed her husband to sleep with her maid, blamed Abraham for Hagar's new attitude when the maid became pregnant, and mistreated Hagar until she ran away. Thirteen years later, Sarah laughed in disbelief when God's messengers said she finally would bear a son at the age of ninety. And when her beloved son, Isaac, was a toddler, Sarah kicked out Hagar and Ishmael to protect Isaac's position in the family.

As you can see, Sarah had some serious lapses in wisdom

and trust, but God was fiercely devoted to her. He never gave up on her, and eventually Sarah indeed became the beloved matriarch of all the Israelites.

Sapphira, on the other hand, was close to the truth and glory of God, but she blew it big time. She and her husband lied to the Holy Spirit, and it cost them their lives. You know the story: They owned some land, sold it, then told the apostles they were donating the full amount to the church, when in fact they kept some money for themselves.

They both lied; they both died. Now, were they inherently bad people? No. Were they wrong to keep some of the money? No. Were they fatally wrong in lying about it? You bet. Sapphira and her husband were there at the beginning of the church, surrounded by people who had walked and talked with Jesus. You know, they probably even met Jesus or heard Him teach. But they missed the point. They didn't trust God to accept them as they were, so they lied to Him.

Woman, wise up and trust God. If you think you can deceive the Maker of our heart, you're only fooling yourself. God knows you intimately. He knows the good and the bad. Accept that love, trust Him, and let Him bring you into destiny.

6 Be of the same mind toward one another.

Do not set your mind on high things,

but associate with the humble.

Do not be wise in your own opinion.

17 Repay no one evil for evil.

Have regard for good things in the sight of all men.

18 If it is possible, as much as depends on you,

live peaceably with all men.

19 Beloved, do not avenge yourselves,

but rather give place to wrath;

for it is written,

"Vengeance is Mine, I will repay,"

says the Lord.

ROMANS 12:16-19

BEING WISE in RELATIONSHIP with OTHERS

He who walks with wise men

will be wise,

But the companion of fools

will be destroyed.

PROVERBS 13:20

O

NCE YOU'VE GOTTEN SOME PERSPECTIVE *on a* RELATIONSHIP *with* GOD,

it's time to take a look at your relationships with other people. Your interactions with other women, your family, your community, and with other believers can have history-shaking consequences.

You show your wisdom in those interactions in two basic ways—how you lead, and how your follow.

That sounds too simple, doesn't it, but stay with me and you'll see what I mean.

Have you ever been part of a good, godly group of women? When you're around them, you get a charge to your spiritual batteries. That's because you're in a situation where you can learn from—or follow—women who have more wisdom in some areas, and then you are able to instruct—or lead—in areas where you have the greater wisdom. And that's good, powerful stuff.

This leading and following gets a little more

complicated when you're talking about relationships with men. In our culture, we've gotten some things out of order when it comes to men and women and their roles. You know what I'm getting to. There's that word "submit" that no one wants to hear, but there's an order that when you understand it, that word "submit" becomes a lot easier to take. A big part of wisdom is learning to live within this order.

In this section, I'm going to show you some women of the Bible who were wise in their relationships with others, plus a few who messed up. I'm also going to elaborate on the order set by God, and if you'll hear me out, some of these times for leading and following will make more sense.

The heart of the prudent

acquires knowledge,

And the ear of the wise

seeks knowledge.

PROVERBS 18:15

NAOMI & RUTH

Their Love Bridged a Big Gap

Women need wisdom from other women. That's a given. As long as there have been women, mothers have taught daughters the essential skills of life. But just having the skills—just being smart—isn't enough. Knowledge must be tempered with wisdom.

There's a story about a young wife who always whacked off the ends of a ham before cooking it. Her husband asked her about it once, and she said that's just how her mother did it. Out of curiosity, she called and asked her mother why she whacked off the ends of the ham. Her mother's response: because her baking pan was too short. You see, the daughter learned the skill of baking a ham, but she didn't learn the wisdom of the process.

In your relationships with other women—no matter how similar or different you are—when you share wisdom with them, when you show them the virtue

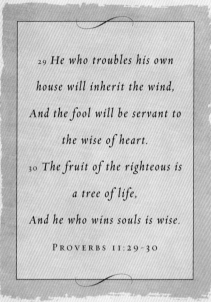

29 *He who troubles his own*

house will inherit the wind,

And the fool will be servant to

the wise of heart.

30 *The fruit of the righteous is*

a tree of life,

And he who wins souls is wise.

PROVERBS 11:29-30

in your character, you are nurturing them to be powerful in the Kingdom.

Turn in your Bible to the book of Ruth and you'll see
what I'm talking about.

You remember the story: A man, his wife, and their
two sons move to a foreign country during hard times at
home in Israel. While there, the sons marry women of that
land, but before any grandchildren come along, the
patriarch and both sons die, leaving three childless widows.

At this time, Naomi, the matriarch, is a foreigner who's
longing to return to her own country. In her bitterness and
grief, she's wise enough to know that it's time to go home.
She needs to be with people who understand and love her.

As much as Naomi loves her Moabite daughters-in-
law, she counsels them to stay there with their own people
and try to find new husbands. She knows that foreigners
aren't very welcome in Israel.

Here's where the daughter-in-law Ruth begins
showing her wisdom. She knows that Naomi is too good to
lose, so Ruth respectfully speaks one of the most-quoted
passages of the Bible:

"Entreat me not to leave you, Or to turn back from following after you; For wherever you go, I will go; And wherever you lodge, I will lodge; Your people shall be my people, And your God, my God. Where you die, I will die, And there will I be buried. The LORD do so to me, and more also, If anything but death parts you and me" (Ruth 1:16-17).

How could Naomi refuse such a request? "So Naomi returned, and Ruth the Moabitess her daughter-in-law with her, who returned from the country of Moab" (Ruth 1:22).

Finally back in Bethlehem after more than a decade away, life was still tough for Naomi. She was a widow who could barely keep a roof over her head, much less feed herself and her foreign daughter-in-law. But they refused to give up, and Ruth humbly offered to take one of the lowest jobs around to keep them from starving.

Ruth caught the attention of Boaz, a wealthy landowner, and he offered her protection and assistance.

So she fell on her face, bowed down to the ground, and said to him, "Why have I found favor in your eyes, that you should take notice of me, since I am a foreigner?" And

Boaz answered and said to her, "It has been fully reported to me, all that you have done for your mother-in-law since the death of your husband, and how you have left your father and your mother and the land of your birth, and have come to a people whom you did not know before. The LORD repay your work, and a full reward be given you by the LORD God of Israel, under whose wings you have come for refuge" (Ruth 2:10-12).

You know how it went from there. Naomi counseled Ruth on how to get Boaz to propose, and it went exactly as Naomi said it would, with Boaz saying, "I will do for you all that you request, for all the people of my town know that you are a virtuous woman" (Ruth 3:11).

So the foreign widow married the Israelite landowner and secured the protection and care that she and Naomi needed. These women's love for each other and their wise, virtuous ways brought them from a miserable existence to a good home. And the bonus that they couldn't have imagined—Ruth's great-grandson was the great King David, an ancestor of the King of Kings, Jesus.

Chances are, ladies, that you're going to run into more and more women from different backgrounds. I'm here to challenge you to love them. These are your sisters. They're cooking dinner, wiping noses, paying bills, and dealing with their men, just like you. The same kinds of things make them smile, sob, dance, or fear.

Whether your differences are age, race, country, attitude, or even faith, you need to be a Naomi looking for a Ruth to nurture. Let them see that you're someone too good to lose, then show them the Source of all goodness and welcome them into the Family. If you're a Ruth, find your Naomi—learn from her, and prepare to be blessed.

The wise shall

inherit glory,

But shame shall be

the legacy of fools.

<small>PROVERBS 3:35</small>

ABIGAIL

Faithful Wife of a Fool

Did you know that some women are married to men who don't appreciate them? Of course you do. You hear it every day on TV, at the store, or from your girlfriend. Maybe you're the one whose husband doesn't know what he's got. It's unfortunate, but we all know it happens.

Even wise women sometimes get not-so-wise men, but they make it work as best as they can.

Abigail was one such wise woman married to a man whose name literally meant "fool." And Nabal lived down to his name, especially when he insulted David.

You see, Nabal was incredibly rich, and although Abigail "was a woman of good understanding and beautiful appearance . . . the man was harsh and evil in his doings" (1 Samuel 25:3).

At the time, David and his army of followers were on the run from King Saul, and they had to live in caves and get by as best they could. One of the ways they got food and supplies was by protecting the property of landowners like Nabal, but when David sent men to ask him for food, Nabal turned them down flat.

Now David wasn't having any of that. He and about four hundred men strapped on their swords and went to do some damage.

But one of Nabal's servants warned Abigail of what her husband had done, even adding, "consider what you will do, for harm is determined against our master and against all his household. For he is such a scoundrel that one cannot speak to him" (1 Samuel 25:17). Abigail packed up a feast for David's army, then raced to head him off. I wonder how many times she practiced her speech on the way, because her wise words and actions saved the day.

Now when Abigail saw David, she dismounted quickly from the donkey, fell on her face before David, and bowed down to the ground. So she fell at his feet and said: "On me, my lord, on me let this iniquity be! And please let your maidservant speak in your ears, and hear the words of your maidservant. Please, let not my lord regard this scoundrel Nabal. For as his name is, so is he: Nabal is his name, and folly is with him! But I, your maidservant, did not see the young men of my lord whom you sent. Now therefore, my lord, as the LORD lives and as your soul lives, since the LORD has held you back from coming to bloodshed and from avenging yourself with your own hand, now then, let your enemies and those who seek harm for my lord be as Nabal. And now this present which your maidservant has brought to my lord, let it be given to the young men who follow my lord. Please forgive the trespass of your maidservant. For the LORD will certainly make for my lord an enduring house, because my lord fights the battles of the LORD, and evil is not found in you throughout your days. Yet a man has risen to pursue you and seek your life, but the life of my lord shall be bound in the bundle of the living with the LORD your God; and the lives of your enemies He shall sling out, as from the pocket of a sling. And it shall come to pass, when the LORD has done for my lord according to all the good that He has spoken concerning you, and has appointed you ruler over Israel, that this will be no grief to you, nor offense of heart to my lord, either that you have shed blood without cause, or that my lord has avenged himself. But when the LORD has dealt well with my lord, then remember your maidservant" (1 Samuel 25:23-31).

Did you see it? Abigail made several appeals to David in one initial burst. She:

- Humbled herself at his feet
- Begged for David to blame her instead for her "scoundrel" husband's actions
- Offered David a way to avoid bloodshed
- Gave generous gifts of food to David and his men
- Begged his forgiveness
- Flattered David for his special favor with the Lord
- Urged David to think ahead and not do something he'd regret

And it worked. David had been intent on killing every male in Nabal's household, but Abigail's fast thinking and decisive action changed his mind.

Abigail had saved her household, and then she faithfully went home to find her husband drunk again. When Nabal sobered up in the morning and Abigail told him what had happened, "his heart died within him, and he became like a stone. Then it happened, after about ten days, that the LORD struck Nabal, and he died" (1 Samuel 25:37-38).

But Abigail wasn't a widow long; as soon as David heard the news, he sent messengers to propose for him, and the wise woman married the anointed king.

Now, God doesn't strike down all foolish husbands. But He does give every woman a chance to be married to a King. God loves you. He wants the best for you.

If you're a wise woman married to a fool, don't assume you can just leave him to his fate. Abigail took care of her household, even though Nabal didn't appreciate her, even though he wasted his life and was a shame to his community. She was faithful, and she was wise. And she saw that commitment through. Then, when the king came along, she was ready to serve and follow him.

Woman, are you faithful enough to see your commitments through? And are you wise enough to serve and follow your King? He's here for you now.

7 The law of the LORD is perfect,

converting the soul;

The testimony of the LORD is sure,

making wise the simple;

8 The statutes of the LORD are right,

rejoicing the heart;

The commandment of the LORD is pure,

enlightening the eyes;

9 The fear of the LORD is clean,

enduring forever;

The judgments of the LORD are true

and righteous altogether.

10 More to be desired are they than gold,

Yea, than much fine gold;

Sweeter also than honey

and the honeycomb

PSALM 19:7-10

DEBORAH

She Spoke for God

In a time when "the Israelites once again did evil in the eyes of the LORD" (Judges 4:1) God let a neighboring king dominate them. After twenty years of suffering, they finally called out to God for help. And of course, God answered them, but His answer was a little different than usual—for the only time in the Old Testament days, He sent a woman to lead them.

We don't know much about Deborah's personal life other than the fact that she was "the wife of Lappidoth" (Judges 4:4) and that she was "a mother in Israel" (Judges 5:7).

What we do know is that she was a prophetess and that "she was leading Israel at that time. She held court under the Palm of Deborah . . . and the Israelites came to her to have their disputes decided" (Judges 4:4-5).

Now, do you know what a prophet is? In our culture we've gotten used to it meaning "someone who can see the future," but that isn't right. "Prophet" is basically another word for "mouthpiece." When the Israelites called Deborah a prophetess, they were saying that they knew she could speak for the Lord. The people relied upon her wisdom, and they knew her words were true.

When the time for deliverance from their enemy came, Deborah sent for Barak to come to her, and her word was so strong that this man—this chosen general—obeyed. She told Barak that God Himself had set the strategy and would ensure the victory, but Barak hesitated. He doubted. He told Deborah, "If you go with me, I will go; but if you don't go with me, I won't go" (Judges 4:8).

Now, Deborah had given her word as a judge and prophetess that the Lord would be with Barak, so she—frustrated, I'm sure—told Barak that although they would still win, he would not have the honor of killing the enemy commander. Instead, that task would fall to a woman.

It's quite telling that although technically Barak was the general, Deborah was the one who gave the order to start the battle. And just as the judge said, the battle ended with the woman Jael killing the enemy general, Sisera.

In the celebration after the victory, Deborah got top

billing in the victory song because Barak had been weak in his heart when he heard God's command.

But what I find fascinating is how the victory song starts. "When the princes of Israel take the lead, when the people willingly offer themselves—praise the LORD" (Judges 5:2).

Did you see it? "When the *princes* of Israel take the lead . . . praise the LORD." Even though Deborah was doing a great job, even though she led Israel to victory, something was off. Israel was supposed to be led by its princes, but because the men were so weak, God changed the order of things and called a woman to get things back on track. He called a woman who was wise and strong, and she came through for the nation. She started waking up Israel's weak men and showed them what was possible with God's help. And after the victory "the land had peace for forty years" (Judges 5:31).

There are a lot of weak men out there today, and things are out of order in our families, in our churches, in our communities, in our nation. Women are having to pick up burdens they were never meant to bear. We have a lot of Deborahs who are doing a great job, but this isn't how it's supposed to be.

Deborah, I know you're frustrated by the Baraks in your life, but don't give up on men. If you're married, keep working gently on your husband; if you're single, hold out for a prince to lead your household.

Wisdom is the right use of
knowledge. To know is not
to be wise . . . There is no fool
so great as the knowing fool.
But to know how to use
knowledge is to have wisdom.

CHARLES SPURGEON
English preacher (1834-1892)

MEN & WOMEN

Same Essence, Different Functions

Few people stop to realize the purpose of marriage as stated in the early pages of the Bible. "Therefore a man shall leave his father and mother and be joined to his wife, and they shall become one flesh" (Genesis 2:24). Here's what many men don't see—and probably women don't either.

Marriage is a partnership in God. It means that it takes two people to make one perfect, loving, and wise individual. When seen from the biblical perspective, it's not intended that a woman threaten a man, but that she be there to help him, to show him things he can't see by himself. God divinely designed it for the two people to come together and to become a whole person.

I've heard it said that opposites attract. I think a better way to say it is that men yearn for women who supply what they lack in their lives, and women need the men who make them complete. This may sound like strange arithmetic, but God says one plus one equals one.

Women are not often considered wise. I think there are reasons for this. Too much emphasis goes on educating women today—and I'm all for that—but our culture is educating them to be smart so they can compete with men. Wise women don't have to compete. They only have to be who God called them to be.

Many smart women get into competition, then end up depressed, feeling worthless, and wondering if they're any good to God or to anyone else. That happens because they focus on the wrong issues.

Why do men and women argue all the time? Because they're smart, but they're not wise.

I'm not coming out against education, and I encourage women to get all the schooling they can. The trouble is that instead of women figuring out who they are—and Whom they belong to and what God wants them to do—they focus on competing, on getting ahead in the office or factory or classroom. "I just can't find my purpose," they cry. They started with the wrong equation, so how can they end up with the right answers?

Wisdom is found on the lips

of him who has understanding,

But a rod is for the back of him

who is devoid of understanding.

Wise people store up knowledge,

But the mouth of the foolish

is near destruction.

PROVERBS 10:13-14

When God created woman, her desire was only for God. Eve was fulfilled in Him. But out of the Garden, woman desired man.

Let's look where this started—and it really did start with Eve. But what happened in the garden wasn't totally her fault.

Before the creation of the woman, God gave Adam two simple instructions. First, He told him what he could do and then what he couldn't: "Of every tree of the garden you may freely eat; but the tree of the knowledge of good and evil you shall not eat" (Genesis 2:19–20).

I want to make this clear. God told *Adam* not to eat from the tree. That means Eve wasn't present when God commanded the man. The only way Eve could get her information was from Adam. For me, this proves something many women know from experience—the man was a poor communicator. At least we have no record of his saying, "Now, Eve, leave that tree alone."

Here's another thing: Adam wasn't around when the devil spoke to Eve. I don't know where he was, but he wasn't home. This makes the obvious point to me that, even today, the devil talks to a lot of women because their husbands aren't home to talk to them.

Man, if we're going to be Adam, we're given charge to instruct Eve. Eve, you're to listen.

It's called communication and it has to go both ways. God's purpose was (and still is) to make the husband and wife into one person. How could that be possible if they don't pass the information freely between them?

Because Adam wasn't there, Eve was susceptible to the cunning words of the devil. If he had been there and communicated, Eve wouldn't have eaten the fruit. I'll say it this way for us today: Where there's not a godly man around, whom will a woman talk to? She'll listen to the devil or to the devil's children.

Eve listened and she ate—and Adam still wasn't around. What did Eve learn between the time she ate and the time Adam came back? She learned the difference between good and evil. If I understand the story properly, she also learned how to manipulate her husband. She ate the fruit, liked it, and said, "Have a bite. It's really good."

And he ate. Adam, who knew better, took the fruit from her hand and ate. Then he received quite a revelation too. He knew he had become a sinner.

As soon as Eve ate it, she got a revelation that Adam didn't have and instead of keeping Adam from eating it, she included him in her sin. Call it manipulation or call it influence or persuasion, but it makes us aware of the power God endowed women with. They have power with men that can build them up or they can use it to manipulate them into sin.

In the Kingdom, we need wise women who won't use their power to manipulate, but to lead us in. Woman, you can be smart, but don't let your smartness overrule your wisdom.

Eve's manipulation doesn't make Adam innocent—he's still responsible.

Let's take the next step. Why did Adam eat? I suggest that Adam already knew he messed up *before* he ate. It had been his responsibility to inform Eve. If he had done what he was supposed to do, she wouldn't have eaten. God had said clearly to Adam: "…for in the day

5 *A wise man will hear and*
increase learning,
And a man of understanding will
attain wise counsel,
6 *To understand a proverb*
and an enigma,
The words of the wise
and their riddles.
7 *The fear of the* LORD *is the*
beginning of knowledge,
But fools despise wisdom
and instruction.

PROVERBS 1:5-7

that you eat of it you shall surely die" (Genesis 2:17).

Adam failed his wife. He didn't follow through on what God had told him. In fact, I want to say this stronger. Eve's death began the moment she bit into the fruit. She died spiritually and would eventually die physically. My assumption is that Adam realized what had happened to his wife—his helper, the person who enabled him to be a complete person. As he saw the difference in her, he must have thought, I'm going to live throughout eternity and Eve is about to die. Then I'll be alone again, just as I was before God created Eve. I don't want that, so I might as well eat with her.

The Bible makes it clear what went on. The devil told Eve that if she ate, she would be like God himself, but the real temptation came when she stared at the fruit. "So when the woman saw the tree was good for food, that it was pleasant to the eyes, and a tree desirable to make one wise, she took of its fruit and ate . . ." (Genesis 3:6).

Eve saw three things. First, it was good for food. I think this appeals to a woman's natural instinct to provide for herself and, even more, for her family. This food would be a wonderful source of provision.

Second, it was pleasant to the eye. Again, I think this is basic to a woman's nature. They want to look good, and they're caught up in personal appearance. One easy way to see this is to realize that today women buy far more clothes for themselves than they do for their husbands (or their husbands buy for themselves) and we don't even have to get on the topic of makeup and perfumes either.

Third, by eating the fruit, it would make her a wise woman. She would know all things. It could imply that she wouldn't have to depend on Adam if he failed her. She simply wanted to know.

Eve saw provision, beauty, and wisdom when the devil tempted her, and she did the most natural thing in the world. She ate. It was just that simple, because she had looked only at what she would gain.

She had not considered what she would lose in the process. She would know the good, but she would also know the ugly.

Now here's the order, as laid down in the Garden.

When God confronted the first sinners, He called Adam first.

Sisters, the reason why God drives home submitting to your husband is because if anything's messed up, God's going to him first. He is responsible. Then, He'll deal with you. It is the husband's responsibility to sanctify his wife, pull her out of the world and use the Word of God—the order of God—to show her who she is, call her into destiny, and bring her into everything that God has ordained.

That's Kingdom order.

Do you see now why that "submit" word isn't so bad? God wouldn't degrade His most awesome creation—He's actually trying to protect you.

13Who is wise and understanding among you?

Let him show by good conduct

that his works are done in the meekness of wisdom.

14 But if you have bitter envy and self-seeking in your hearts,

do not boast and lie against the truth.

15 This wisdom does not descend from above,

but is earthly, sensual, demonic.

16 For where envy and self-seeking exist,

confusion and every evil thing are there.

17 But the wisdom that is from above is first pure,

then peaceable, gentle, willing to yield,

full of mercy and good fruits,

without partiality and without hypocrisy.

18 Now the fruit of righteousness is sown in peace

by those who make peace.

JAMES 3:13-18

the WISE WOMAN of TEKOA

She Changed the Course of a King

One of my favorite wise women in the Bible isn't even named, but she changed the mind of King David of Israel. Her wisdom impacted official policy of the land and reunited a father and son, if only for a while.

After David became the king of Israel, he made a few serious mistakes. In particular, we read in the Bible that although he excelled at almost everything— shepherd, musician, poet, warrior, statesman—David was a lousy father. He seemed to have little interest in his many children. If he had been a faithful father who actively loved and disciplined his children, the great tragedies of his reign would not have happened.

One of David's sons, Amnon, raped his half-sister Tamar. After waiting two years while David did nothing to punish Amnon, another of David's sons, Absalom, took the law into his own hands and had the rapist killed. Absalom then fled into exile. This series of family tragedies set up a chain of events that led to the deaths of thousands of people.

David mourned the loss of Absalom, but he was unable to reach out to his beloved son, forgive him, and invite him back.

Joab, the wily captain of David's army, realized how deeply the king grieved over the great rift with Absalom, so he crafted a plan to reconcile the father and son.

Here's the way the Bible tells it:

So Joab, the son of Zeruiah perceived that the king's heart was concerned about Absalom and Joab sent to Tekoa and brought from there a wise woman. And said to her, "Please pretend to be a mourner and put on mourning apparel and do not anoint yourself with oil but act like a woman who has been mourning a long time for the dead. Go to the king and speak to him in this manner." So Joab put the words in her mouth (2 Samuel 14:1–2).

For his plan to work, Joab had to have an

accomplice—a woman. Please notice that Joab didn't pick just any woman. The Bible says he searched and brought from Tekoa *a wise woman.*

It is true, of course, that Joab coached her on what to say to David, but the woman's wisdom and ability to improvise were eventually what made the plan work.

The story goes like this. The wise woman gets an audience with King David. Although the Bible doesn't explain how she, a common person, could appeal to the king, most scholars think that King David sat as the appeal judge in serious cases. The story the wise woman brings before him involves murder and retribution—making it a capital offense—and the kind where only the king could reverse the decision of the judges.

The woman, using an invented tale, of course, comes before the king as if to say, "I appeal to you to overturn the decision of the judge and give me justice."

Here's the story if I were to write the Bishop Long version. The wise woman waits until the king holds out his scepter to her. To show her utter respect for the king, she falls down a dozen feet in front of his throne

10 *The fear of the* LORD *is the beginning of wisdom, And the knowledge of the Holy One is understanding.* 11 *For by me your days will be multiplied, And years of life will be added to you.* 12 *If you are wise, you are wise for yourself, And if you scoff, you will bear it alone."*

PROVERBS 9:10-12

and slowly crawls forward, head down. She sobs, wails, and finally moans, "Help me, King! Help me!" David, sitting on his throne and touched by her many tears, extends a benevolent hand toward her and says, "What's brothering you, mother in Israel? Why are you so upset?"

Now the wise woman goes into playing the grief-stricken mother. "I'm a poor, lowly widow, and I have no one to come to my aid. The judge has ruled against me. My husband is dead. My relatives only care about taking away the little I have. You, O wise and mighty king, are my only hope."

She holds the king's attention, so she spells out her story. "O great king, you are a father and you understand how boys can quarrel and not get along."

"Oh, yes, such things happen all the time. Boys will be boys."

"That is how it happened in this case. Except they were not small, but grown into manhood, both of them. O great king, I had only two sons. One day my two sons disagreed over something—I never even knew what it was. I heard their voices as they yelled at each other. Each was convinced that the other had done him wrong."

She pauses to cry for a minute and then wipes away her tears. "The worst thing imaginable happened. My older son killed my younger son."

With frequent pauses for her wails of pain, the wise woman explains that elders grabbed the surviving son and imprisoned him until they could have a trial. At the court hearing, which lasted only minutes, "The judge declared that my son—my now only surviving son—is a murderer. As a murderer he must be put to death."

She pauses again for fresh wails of grief. "Oh, yes, great king, that is justice and I could not argue with that. But he is my only son, great king."

So far, aside from her sadness, she knows she has not made a case for him to reverse. In her powerful wisdom she has been setting up the king to softly influence him into doing what she wants.

"I cried out to my relatives and begged for mercy, but they would not listen. 'He has murdered his brother and he must pay,' they said and scorned my plea for mercy." The wise woman crawls two feet closer to the king until she is able to touch his feet. She clasps them with her hands. All the time, she keeps her head low, for she knows she is never allowed to gaze into the eyes of the ruler. "Oh, do not let this happen, my king. If they kill this son—my one surviving child—there is none left. Then we will have no one to carry on the family name and our line will die."

This may seem complex to moderns, but the gist is that her son was guilty of manslaughter. If he paid the just penalty—being put to death—the mother would suffer, too, and it would be worse than suffering the loss of another son. The law provided for the forfeiture of all their property; it would be turned over for other relatives to inherit. She, as a widow, had no property rights; they could take everything, and that would leave her destitute.

The wise woman slowly brings the king around and makes her point of sparing the young man's life.

Let's compare that with Absalom's situation. By now David and those in power knew the circumstances of Tamar's rape, David's refusal to do anything, and the revenge exacted before Absalom fled the country. Absalom had acted wrongly in killing his half-brother, but they also knew Absalom had had a just quarrel with Amnon. They were aware that David had done nothing to Amnon, who had raped his virginal half-sister.

David was not only a king, but he was a king with vast power and influence. He could easily have sent an ambassador and a small garrison of troops and asked the king of Geshur to return Absalom. That would have been neither unusual nor difficult.

But David, again, had done nothing.

The one difference—and here is where the wisdom of the woman lies—is that David loves Absalom. She will use her wisdom to remind David of his deep affection for Absalom.

David is leaning forward, totally caught up in the misery of the woman. He responds with a clenched fist and a solemn oath.

"As the Lord lives, not one hair of your son shall fall to the ground" (2 Samuel 14:11).

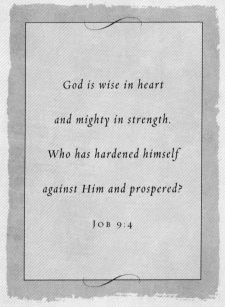

God is wise in heart

and mighty in strength.

Who has hardened himself

against Him and prospered?

JOB 9:4

David has been hooked. She's now ready to give him the payoff as the true wisdom flows from the woman's mouth. She crawls another three inches forward. "I am not worthy to say more," I can hear her say, "but oh my king, do not be angry but only allow me to say this one thing more."

"Speak up, mother in Israel. Speak up, for I've already shown you that I'm a kind and merciful king."

In the Bishop Long version, the woman now dares to raise her head and she stares into the dark brown eyes of the king. "Thank you for this justice, for setting the wrongs to rights. Now, oh king, because you have given me permission to speak, I will ask you one question." I can see her eyes gleam as she focuses totally on his face.

"Yes, say on."

"Why then have you schemed such a thing against the people of God? For the king speaks this thing as one who is guilty" (2 Samuel 14:13).

"What are you talking about?" replies the shocked monarch. "How have I schemed? How have I done evil?"

"You are guilty, great king. Remember that you have

promised mercy, my great king. But listen. You have a banished son and you refuse to forgive him. You make him stay in exile, and you will not bring him home."

Then the wise woman speaks poetically to make him know that it pleases God to save lives and not to take them. "You would show deep kindness to me, a widow in Israel. For that I am grateful. Yet you will do nothing for your own flesh and blood. You have a son, whom you love dearly and who is loved by all of us, your loyal subjects, and yet he is not allowed to be among us."

A shocked monarch stares at her as the words sink in.

This wise woman isn't finished. "The word of my lord the king will now be comforting; for as the angel of God, so is my lord the king in discerning good and evil. And may the LORD your God be with you" (2 Samuel 14:17).

As David listens to all of this, and being no fool himself, he perceives not only what the woman wants, but he's smart enough to figure out that someone else has put the woman up to this. There's only one man in the kingdom who would dare to try such a bold gesture.

"Tell me, woman," he says, and holds out his hand

to show his sincerity, "tell me who put you up to this. Surely, this isn't something you thought of yourself. You didn't come here on your own to take this risk of offending me."

In my version, her lips tremble—not that she's really afraid, but this is the wise woman doing her best acting. "Oh, sir, no, no I—"

"Joab is behind this, is he not? Don't be afraid to speak the truth to me."

Again, she uses wisely chosen words to answer: "As you live, my lord the king, no one can turn to the right hand or to the left from anything that my lord the king has spoken" (2 Samuel 14:20). Again she flatters David and praises him for being such a perceptive man.

David has lost. The wise woman has defeated the king.

"Bring him home," David says wearily. Although in my version that's how he says it, inside the king rejoices that the wise woman has given him an out.

This wise woman enabled the king to save face. He had been wrong in not doing anything about Amnon and certainly not in following his heart and forgiving

Absalom. This wise woman took him in so completely that she forced him to admit that and, thus, he is able to call for Absalom's return.

If it had not been for the wisdom of that woman, would David ever have acted like a loving father? Would he ever have extended mercy to his son? I don't think he would have.

When the woman went to speak with David she behaved just like Nathan had done when he slyly told David a story about a man with many sheep who killed the single lamb of a poor family. The story enraged David and he threatened to have that rich man executed. "You are the man,"(2 Samuel 12:7) were the accusing words of Nathan as he confronted David with his actions toward Bathsheba and her husband, Uriah.

The wise woman pulled off an outstanding feat just as Joab had coached her. Joab's problem had been to find a way to bring Absalom back and not directly confront the king. That is why he sought for and found the wise woman.

I also want to point out that God used the wise

woman to do what a man couldn't do. Too many men—back then and even today—put so much into masculine pride, it's difficult for them to admit a mistake. For such men, the one sentence they never say is, "I was wrong."

Even David found it wrong to admit his all failings. For instance, when God convicted David of sin with Bathsheba, he fell on his face and wept, but when it came to his dealings with others, and especially the matter of raising his own children, we don't find him falling on his face and asking for wisdom. I suspect that he was caught somewhere between being a powerful king and a macho man. To say, "I was wrong. I shouldn't have sent Absalom away," was too much for his pride to handle. It was something he simply could not do.

This is a powerful moment in the history of Israel. It's also the power of a wise woman that has brought about many changes and insights in life.

If Rosa Parks

had not sat down,

Martin King would

not have stood up.

U N K N O W N

a WISE WOMAN CAN SAY WHAT a MAN CAN'T

Here's why I believe Joab sought out a wise woman—he knew that only a woman could pull this off. None of his pleading or arguments would make a difference, but the well-chosen wise words of a woman were different.

There are times when most men can't talk to other men. There are times when captains can't speak to the king. There are times when a man has a struggle between what he considers masculine strength and being a wimp. They refuse to yield to the truth even when they know better.

I'll say it stronger. There are times when a man will make a bad decision, and as soon as he announces his decision, he knows it was a mistake. Will he say, "Oh, excuse me, I shouldn't have said that?" No, he usually isn't humble enough.

If that's true for common, ordinary men, how much more difficult must it have been for the king? Here was the head of the nation, the great soldier, and the one who had brought the kingdom of Israel to its highest point. He could not be wrong. He was the king.

Yes, but the king was wrong! His pride wouldn't allow him to acknowledge his errors.

The wise woman comes into the story and does for David what he cannot do for himself. She uses subterfuge, but in that culture she frames it in an acceptable method of getting the truth to people.

She appealed to David by using a parable—a story form—to bring the king around to her way of thinking. In our culture, the person on the receiving end would have been furious, but in those ancient days, however, good parables always contained a surprise ending. Look at the story of the Prodigal Son. It's the unfaithful younger son who suddenly becomes the celebrated one. Consider the parable of the Good Samaritan. The enemy—the alien Samaritan—turns out to be the good guy.

The parable was the only method that would have worked, and in this case, Joab knew he needed a wise woman to pull it off.

And wise women are still saying the right things and

outsmarting men whose minds are closed and so filled with pride they can't face the truth.

Yes, it is still happening. My wife, Vanessa, can say things to me that no man would dare to face me with. She has an intuitive wisdom, a way of being able to say exactly the right word and at just the proper time. It's the time when I'm finally ready to hear the truth, because she says it in a way that makes me able to hear it from her.

When Vanessa tells me the painful truth about myself, I confess that I don't usually shout praises to God. Sometimes I may even momentarily resent what she's made me face, because she has just touched my vulnerable spot. It's as if she's God's love and power at work, forcing me to look at myself and see the things about myself that I don't like and don't want to face. And she has the wisdom to do that in such a loving way, I have to accept what she says.

I also know that Vanessa is not trying to take advantage of me, and she doesn't do it to make me feel weak. She's trying to build me up and make me stronger. Once I understand what her wise words are trying to point out—that is, once I get over my irritation or anger at being told that I've made a serious mistake—I listen.

Not only do I listen to her—and I may still be smarting from what she pushes me to face—but I show I'm listening because I'm bright enough to follow her wisdom. Then, like King David of old, whom the wise woman outsmarted, I'm bright enough to know that Vanessa outmaneuvered the man she was talking to. What we men need are women who care enough about us to use their God-given wisdom to partner with us, to lovingly confront us, and to quietly guide us toward making the right choices and above all, to help us men correct our mistakes.

Like David, sometimes we know what we should do if we follow our hearts, but we hold out and ignore what needs to be done. That masculine pride I've mentioned is so powerful, that we'll blow everything rather than to admit we were wrong. That's when we need the wise woman to speak tenderly and gently to us.

If we are going to take the kingdom of God forward, men need to throw off masculine pride, the macho image, that hard, outer shell, and be able to receive truth from the women in our lives who care enough to tell us the truth about ourselves.

BEING WISE *in* RELATIONSHIP *with* HERSELF

Never be ashamed to own

you have been in the wrong,

'tis but saying

you are wiser today

than you were yesterday.

JONATHAN SWIFT
English poet (1667-1745)

T HERE *is* NOTHING FINER THAN *a* WOMAN WHO KNOWS WHO SHE IS.

A woman who knows who she is will not accept trash, whether that trash is a bad relationship, a lie from the devil, or some other filthy thing.

A woman of God knows that He loves her. She knows that He has appointed her a destiny, she knows that He will provide appropriate human love and support, and she is wise enough to obey His call.

When a woman is walking in her calling, she is a walking epistle to the truth of God. She's powerful.

But woman, your power is not in the volume of your voice. It's not in the mightiness of your actions. Your power is in the preciousness of God knowing who you are—it's the quiet beauty that you have.

Whenever a woman walks in her womanhood, she is qualified to walk with kings, because when you discover who you are, you are automatically a queen.

Let's look at a woman whose queenly character changed history.

20 *Listen to counsel*
and receive instruction,
That you may be wise
in your latter days.
21 *There are many plans*
in a man's heart,
Nevertheless the LORD'S
counsel—that will stand.

PROVERBS 19:20-21

ESTHER

She Embraced Her Destiny

Esther was a beauty whose true power was more than skin deep. You might not be used to thinking of Esther as a wise woman, but she was. Let me show you.

The Jews at the time were captives of the vast Persian Empire, which was ruled by King Xerxes. One night at a feast, Xerxes' queen disobeyed him. Now when a man rules 127 provinces, it looks really bad when his own wife insults him publicly. His advisers warned him that chaos could break out at any minute, so Xerxes deposed his queen and started rounding up new candidates, including the lovely Esther.

Esther's beautiful face got her in the door, but her beautiful character is what won her favor with the king and everyone else who met her.

Queen Esther had a secret, though—she was a Jewess. On the advice of her cousin Mordecai, she was discreet

about her heritage until years after she became queen, when she had to risk her life to save her people. You know that line about her destiny; when she expressed her fear, Mordecai reassured her, "Who knows whether you have come to the kingdom for such a time as this?" (Esther 4:14). How could she not agree? She recognized her destiny and she embraced it.

But what Mordecai *didn't* say is also significant. He told Esther to appeal to the king, but he didn't tell her how to do it. She had to figure that out herself. Mordecai and all her people were relying on her wisdom to keep them alive.

You know what she did. She decked herself out in her best clothes and asked the king and Haman to dinner—the thoughtful gesture of a loving wife. (Of course, the invitation was also bold and intriguing, since Esther could have been killed for approaching the king on her own initiative.) The king offered her whatever she wanted, but she just invited him and Haman to come back for another banquet the next day. And the next day, when the king was feeling relaxed and happy, Esther made her plea: "If I have found favor in your sight, O king, and if it pleases the king, let my life be given me at my petition, and my people at my request. For we have been sold, my people and I, to be destroyed, to be killed, and to be annihilated." (Esther 7:3-4).

Her plan worked. The king hanged Haman and wrote a new law allowing the Jews to protect themselves from the pogram. Instead of being massacred, the Jews won prominence in the kingdom because a wise beauty had the courage to use her gifts.

Esther's beauty was a great gift—but without wisdom, she would have failed.

Ladies, next time you're in front of the mirror, look deeply into your eyes and try to see your inner Esther. Look *into* yourself instead of looking *at* yourself.

If you educate a man,

you educate an individual,

but if you educate a woman,

you educate a nation.

GHANAIAN PROVERB

BEAUTY *is* REALLY HEART-DEEP

One of the things women need to realize is the source of their beauty. I like it when women wear attractive makeup and choose clothes that show off their best qualities. But that's not the same as the beauty the Bible speaks about.

The godly beauty—and the beauty that comes as power through the wise woman—comes from inside. Health spas can help women lose weight or tone their bodies, but they can't give the inner beauty that God speaks about.

The wise woman knows that she begins to become beautiful when she learns who she is in Jesus Christ. She's not getting pretty on the outside to attract a man to fall in love with her. She's getting beautiful inside so that a man who is worthy of her will fall in love with her.

I've never understood why women shortchange themselves. I call woman "God's Better Idea," and "The Mother of All Creation."

When God gets ready to do something, He turns to a woman to have it birthed, nurtured, and brought forth. He does not trust us men with His precious assignments. If I could run through the Bible and give examples of how precious, special, unique, beautiful and how divine God has made woman, it amazes me as a man to know how insecure, how back-shuffling and second-guessing women are when it comes to who they are. Yet they often compare themselves to one another—"as long as I'm better than Sally," as long as I'm better than Susie." Then some women are so insecure that they try to live their lives through somebody else—"If I could just be as pretty or as smart as she is"—and they spend their entire lives trying to be who and what they are not.

When I was a boy, I used to hear people say, "Pretty is as pretty does." That may be an old-fashioned saying, but it has a simple truth. Pretty shows itself in action. And where do those actions come from? They grow out of a good heart and from a right spirit. True prettiness comes from the woman who is wise enough to serve God and discover her inner beauty first.

For those who want to know the power of the wise woman, here's exactly what I think it is—true wisdom comes to women when they love themselves. It comes when they love the person God created them to be.

Ask any woman about her physical beauty, and she'll always find the flaws. But the wise woman concentrates on perfecting her inner beauty.

In fact, I read that a reporter went through a dozen health spas in New York City and asked women this question: "Do you feel you are truly beautiful?" Of the 900 women asked, none of them—not one—ever said, "I am beautiful." When asked why they didn't consider themselves beautiful, they all referred to some defect in their bodies. Their thighs were too flabby was the number one response. The other major responses were that their rear ends were too large or their breasts were too small or too large. Everyone had a defect. None

A fool vents all his feelings,

But a wise man

holds them back.

PROVERBS. 29:11

of them was beautiful—to herself.

As I read that, I thought, as long as you put all the emphasis on the outside, you'll only see defects when you stare at the mirror. But if you find true inner beauty, you don't worry about any physical flaw.

I'll tell you something else. We all know that beauty fades. For the first forty or so years of their lives, women invest all that time, all that effort, all those expensive clothes and hair styles into physical beauty. Then, by the time their hair starts turning gray, they're in a state of panic because now they have to add *old* to their list of physical flaws.

That's not true of the really wise women, and that's why they have such power. They know who they are. They're wise enough to know that physical beauty won't last, but inner beauty only increases as the years go by.

The wise woman, aware of her inner beauty and her relationship to Jesus Christ can say, "When you look at me you see the original." She's not trying to be somebody else, and she's not trying to make her beauty begin on the outside.

Peter understood this principle. In chapter 3 of his

first letter, he directs a portion of his message to women. He counsels them on how to win their husbands to Christ—that is, he's showing them how to be wise. He says that by their conduct they can win the men in their lives. Peter is giving the simplest advice—and the wise woman listens. He says that she is to be a good wife. By her silent preaching through the loveliness of her life, she might break down the barriers of hostility and win her husband to the Lord.

Peter also tells her to be submissive, and I don't believe that means a cringing and spineless submission. I like to think of it as a voluntary selflessness. It means she has the wisdom to know that if she puts her husband first in her life, he'll adore her. If she becomes the woman he needs to make him a full person, he'll value her wisdom and turn to her more than ever.

Her submissiveness means that she's so filled with inner beauty—that is, the love of Jesus Christ—that she has no problems with pride and she desires to serve her husband. She doesn't do the service out of fear of being beaten if she doesn't, but out of an awe of God and out of deep love that

God gives her for her mate.

The wise woman is pure—she is faithful to her husband because she knows being faithful to him is being faithful to God. God didn't call her to be part of a threesome, but to be one with her husband. Then together they would be a couple with God. A wise woman's beauty is also reverent. She lives in the conviction that God is in charge of the entire world. As she understands that and as her way of life manifests that reverence, her inner beauty shines for those around her.

Peter goes on to talk about beauty: "Do not let your beauty be that outward adorning of arranging the hair, or wearing gold, or of putting on fine apparel, but let it be the hidden person of the heart, with the incorruptible ornament of a gentle and quiet spirit, which is very precious in the sight of God" (1 Peter 3:4–5).

Too many people have misinterpreted or misapplied that verse. There was a time when I was a boy that I could walk down any street and could almost always pick out Christian women. They wore no makeup, didn't do anything to their hair, and never wore jewelry of any kind. I won't say they were ugly to the eyes, but I'll say that they sure could have used a little help so that the outer beauty matched with the inner beauty.

For too long, some believers tried to make this read that Peter forbade women from doing anything to make themselves attractive. That's not what he was writing. He was stating the very principle I've been emphasizing. He was saying, "Don't find your beauty through hairstyles, jewelry, or revealing clothing. Find your beauty find within."

In fact, maybe it's because some women have no sense of inner beauty that they *have to* spend so much time, money, and effort in trying to make themselves look good outwardly.

The Bible never says women shouldn't look their best. The commands and warnings are always to prevent them from putting the emphasis in the wrong place—looking beautiful outside and being hideous on the inside.

Peter pleads for the graces that adorn the heart. He yearns for the gentle and quiet spirit. He says that the godly women of old adorned themselves with a gentle and

I have done according

to your words; see,

I have given you a wise

and understanding heart,

so that there has not been

anyone like you before you,

nor shall any like you

arise after you.

1 KINGS 3:12

quiet spirit. Then he goes on to cite Sarah as an example.

He holds up Sarah as a role model—we've already seen how Sarah sometimes didn't trust God, but we also know she was very strong. She didn't sit around and let Abraham run over her, and she was a vital part of her husband's life and destiny. Peter holds her up as an example, and then he adds for the women, ". . . whose daughters you are if you do good and are not afraid with any terror" (1 Peter 3:6).

I won't take time to go into it, but Peter next addresses men and lays just as strong a burden on husbands on how they are to treat their wives. It's obvious that Peter is leading up to a point—the oneness in the relationship. In fact, he ends the verse to husbands with words to admonish them to live peacefully with their wives "as heirs together of the grace of life, that your prayers may not be hindered" (1 Peter 3:7).

Earlier I referred to God's purpose for marriage— that a man and a woman were joined by God to become one. Now Peter is showing the results of the unity. If they are truly one in their faith, God will answer their prayers.

If the husbands don't treat their wives properly, their prayers will be hindered—God just won't answer. The implication is there that the same applies to women.

Wise women don't even have to read that admonition to their husbands. They know it already. If they strive for inner beauty, it shows on the outside. And if it shows on the outside, that means their conduct will please God, and they will live in harmony with their husbands.

₂ The tongue of the wise uses knowledge rightly,

But the mouth of fools pours forth foolishness.

₃ The eyes of the LORD are in every place,

Keeping watch on the evil and the good.

₄ A wholesome tongue is a tree of life,

But perverseness in it breaks the spirit.

₅ A fool despises his father's instruction,

But he who receives correction is prudent.

₆ In the house of the righteous there is much treasure,

But in the revenue of the wicked is trouble.

₇ The lips of the wise disperse knowledge,

But the heart of the fool does not do so.

PROVERBS 15:2-7

the VIRTUOUS WOMAN

A Model to Strive For

One of the best ways to see a wise woman is to look in Proverbs, especially in the passage at Proverbs 31:10–31.

We can't see this in English, but in Hebrew those verses were written as an acrostic. Each verse began with one of the twenty-two letters of the Hebrew alphabet. The reason I point this out is because the acrostic made the passage easier to memorize. It also explains why the material jumps around and doesn't always follow a logical order, at least to our eyes. By using the acrostic, however, a Hebrew man could memorize it as he sought for a wise and godly woman. A woman could memorize it as she sought to become that kind of woman.

Proverbs 31:12 says of the godly woman that for her husband "she does him good and not evil." That may well be a reminder of what Eve did and the writer put it there as a warning to women of the future.

The wise and godly woman works hard. We read one statement after another about her industriousness. Then the Scriptures say that "Her children rise up and call her blessed; her husband also, and he praises her" (Proverbs 31:28). For instance, it says in Proverbs 31:27 that she didn't eat the bread of idleness. That's an understatement. "She also rises while it is yet night" (Proverbs 31:15), works all day, and then stays at her tasks until late. "Her lamp does not go out by night" (Proverbs 31:18).

Her work seems overwhelming, but there is no word of complaint as she cooks, makes clothes from raw materials, and even conducts business. "She considers a field and buys it; from her profits she plants a vineyard" (Proverbs 31:16). This shows great wisdom, because she thinks the situation through carefully. She had worked hard for her money and she invests it wisely.

What is this trying to say to us? There is power in a wise woman. She can hold her own in a man's world. She isn't competing, and everything she does is for the family, but she uses the wisdom that God gave her for the benefit of her family. She knows how to drive a hard bargain and has the wisdom to know how to use the money well.

To give a fuller picture of this wise woman, she also has a good heart. "She extends her hand to the poor. Yes, she reaches out her hands to the needy" (Proverbs 31:20).

I'll tell you what I like best about this woman—she listens and she cares. "She opens her mouth with wisdom; and on her tongue is the law of kindness" (Proverbs 31:26). This is a poetic way to say that this woman shows the mercy of God when she goes to people in need. She listens to their problems and needs.

And what kind of words come out when she finally speaks? She doesn't stir up strife or cause problems. Instead, her words ring with wisdom.

This tells us why the wise woman is godly and why there is power in her wisdom. She doesn't try to control, manipulate, or demand. She listens to people, and she also listens for God to speak to her—to give her exactly the right words to say for that moment.

When we speak about wisdom,

we are speaking of Christ.

When we speak about virtue,

we are speaking of Christ.

When we speak about justice,

we are speaking of Christ.

When we speak about peace,

we are speaking of Christ.

When we speak about truth

and life and redemption,

we are speaking of Christ.

AMBROSE
Bishop of Milan (340-397)

the POWER
of a WISE
WOMAN

There is no limit

to the power

of a good woman.

ROBERT HUGH BENSON,
English Roman Catholic Monsignor
(1871-1914)

SISTERS *in* CHRIST, YOU HAVEN'T BEEN CALLED *to be* LIKE OTHER WOMEN.

God has a higher standard for you. What He has called you to do will go from generation to generation. He asks you to surpass your circumstances so He can tell you what is in your being to birth into His Kingdom and what He has called you to nurture into fullness.

Single or married, young or old, educated or uneducated, large or skinny, when you realize who you are in Christ, then you'll realize your awesome wisdom and power. You'll never be the same, and neither will your world.

When does a woman walk into true womanhood? When she accepts responsibility for what God has billed to her. All God's destined blessings fall into place from there.

A home

without a mother

is a desert.

ERITREAN PROVERB

TO LEARN MORE

When Eddie Long became the pastor of New Birth Missionary Baptist Church in Atlanta, it had a membership of 300. Under this leadership it has grown to more than 24,000, with members being added daily. Bishop Long and his wife, Vanessa, have four children.

For more information about Bishop Eddie Long or the congregation he serves, go to www.bellmins.com or www.newbirth.org.

OTHER BOOKS BY EDDIE LONG

What a Man Wants, What a Woman Needs

"Our beliefs about what makes a male a man and what makes a female a woman impact every area of our life," observes Bishop Eddie L. Long. If you are tired of the failure that comes from conforming to the world's model for relationships, *What a Man Wants, What a Woman Needs* will equip and guide you in building successful Kingdom relationships that release the greatness God has in store for you, your family, and your church.

Called to Conquer

In this 365-day devotional, each Biblically-based page contains a Scripture reading, a commentary, and a short prayer. The same robust and energetic style that makes Bishop Long a popular minister will also draw the reader into the pages of this book.